The Our Father and the Hail Mary

By
Rev. Lawrence G. Lovasik, S.V.D.
Divine Word Missionary

Catholic Book Publishing Corp., New Jersey

The OUR FATHER

ONE day the Apostles said to Jesus: "Lord, teach us how to pray, as John taught his disciples." Jesus told them: "When you pray, say as follows:

"Our Father, Who art in heaven,
hallowed be Thy Name.
Thy Kingdom come.
Thy will be done on earth
as it is in heaven.
Give us this day our daily bread;
and forgive us our trespasses
as we forgive those who trespass
   against us.
And lead us not into temptation,
but deliver us from evil."

2

NIHIL OBSTAT; Daniel V. Flynn, J.C.D., *Censor Librorum*
IMPRIMATUR: ✠ Joseph T. O'Keefe, D.D., *Vicar General, Archdiocese of New York*

CPSIA   December 2013   10 9 8 7 6 5 4   A/P

© 1985 by *Catholic Book Publishing Corp., N.Y.* – Printed in Hong Kong   ISBN 978-0-89942-389-0

Jesus teaches the Apostles the "Our Father."

THE Our Father is also called the Lord's Prayer because Jesus Himself taught it to the Apostles.

There is no better or holier prayer. It fits the needs of everybody. It contains all that we, as children of God, can and should ask God for, to help us in soul and body.

We do not only ask God for what is good for us, but we also put the most important thing first. We ask first for God's glory, and then for help in our needs.

Our Father, Who Art in Heaven

MY God in heaven, I call You my Father,
    because You created me;
    because Your Son became our Brother
    when He was made man,
    and we are all brothers and sisters;
    and because at Baptism
    the Holy Spirit made me Your child
    and came to live in my soul.

I want to call You "Father"
    because the word fills my soul
    with love and trust in You.

Though You are everywhere,
    Your throne is in heaven,
    and only there do the Angels and Saints
    see You as You are.

Give me childlike love and trust in You,
    that I may always be with You by Your grace
    and see You face to face in heaven.

Before the "Our Father" in the Mass, the priest says:
**"Through Jesus, with Him, and in Him,
in the unity of the Holy Spirit,
all glory and honor is Yours, almighty Father, forever!"**

6

Hallowed Be Thy Name

HEAVENLY Father, You glorified Your Name when You created Angels, people, and the world.

You glorified Your name again
   when You redeemed the human race
   through the death and resurrection of Your
      Son.

On the night before He died to save the world,
   Jesus prayed to You: "Father, glorify Your
      Name."

You answered from heaven:
   "I have both glorified it and will glorify it
      again."

Father in heaven,
   may Your Name be honored by all people!

May I honor Your name all my life
   by doing all things for Your honor
   and for love of You.

Thy Kingdom Come!

HEAVENLY Father, may Your Kingdom come
  on earth!

I pray that You may be known and loved
  and served on earth.

I pray that the Catholic Church may spread
  throughout the world, especially in pagan
  countries.

I pray that through sanctifying grace,
  your Holy Trinity—Father, Son and Holy
  Spirit—
  may live in more Christian souls as in a temple,
  for Jesus said: "The Kingdom of God is
  within you."

Jesus Christ, my Savior,
  may Your Kingdom come for us,
  the Kingdom promised us by the Father.

Jesus, reign over us as our King
  in the Holy Sacrament of the Altar,
  and in our hearts.

"Sacred Heart of Jesus, Your Kingdom come!" **9**

Thy Will Be Done on Earth
As It Is in Heaven

HEAVENLY Father, I ask for the grace
    to do Your will on earth
  as the Angels and Saints do it in heaven.

Let me do Your will
    by obeying Your Ten Commandments
    and the Laws of Your Church;
    by accepting everything that happens to me
    because I know that You allowed it to hap-
        pen.

You are my Father,
    and You know what is best for me.
    You love me with a love that has no limit.
    I honor You when I do Your will.

In all my prayers,
    and especially in all my sufferings,
    I always want to say: "Thy will be done!"

Jesus said: "If a man wishes to come after Me, he must deny his very self, take up his cross, and follow in My footsteps" (Mk 8, 34).

Give Us This Day Our Daily Bread

MY heavenly Father, Jesus taught me to pray to You,
because You are my Father.
You love Your children and want them to be happy in this world and in heaven.

Jesus said: "Your Father in heaven
knows you have need of all these things. . . .
Whatever you ask the Father in My Name
He will give you.
Ask and you shall receive."

I ask You, Father,
for all that I need for life here on earth,
such as food, clothing, work, health, and true happiness.

I also ask for the daily Bread
of Holy Communion.
For Jesus said: "I am the Bread of Life."

May that Bread give me eternal life with You
as Jesus promised.

Jesus said, "I myself am the living bread come down from heaven. If anyone eats this bread he shall live forever" (Jn 6, 51).

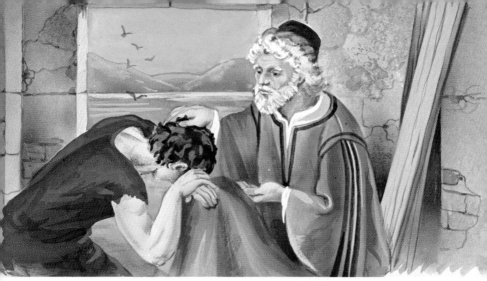

The younger son returned and said,
"Father, I have sinned!"

And Forgive Us Our Trespasses

HEAVENLY Father, I believe
   that sin is the greatest evil in the world
because a serious sin makes me fail
in my love for You,
   and turns me away from doing Your will.

But I also believe
   that You are merciful and will pardon me
   if I am truly sorry for my sins
   because they offend You,
   my loving Father and Highest Good.

God gives us his forgiveness in the Sacrament of Penance.

As We Forgive Those Who Trespass Against Us

I BELIEVE that in the Sacrament of Penance
Jesus comes to forgive my sins
and brings peace with You, my God,
and with the Church, which is hurt by my
sins.

Heavenly Father, on the Cross Jesus prayed:
"Father, forgive them for they do not know
what they are doing."

As Jesus forgave those who put Him to death,
help me to forgive those who hurt me.
Only then can I expect You to forgive me.

Jesus said to the devil: "Away with you, Satan!"

And Lead Us Not into Temptation

HEAVENLY Father, Jesus, Your Son,
   was tempted in the desert.
His prayer gave Him strength to overcome
   the devil who tried to make Him do
   what was against Your holy will.

I also ask You to help me
   when the devil tempts me to do bad things.
Keep me from the persons, places, and things
   that lead me into sin.

God gave me a Guardian Angel to protect me.

But Deliver Us from Evil

HEAVENLY Father, I ask You to protect me
  from evil—
from everything that may be harmful
such as sickness, accidents, and poverty.
Keep me in Your loving care,
and send Your Angels to protect me.

But I ask You to protect me
  from the greatest evil in the world—sin!
Help me to be sorry for my past sins
and to resist temptation in the future.

The "Our Father" in The Mass

HEAVENLY Father, I believe that the "Our Father"—the prayer Jesus taught us,— is never more powerful than when it is said with Jesus at Holy Mass.

18   In the Mass Jesus is our Best Gift to the Father, and our Best Gift from the Father in Holy Communion.

I believe that the sacrifice of Calvary
   is offered again in an unbloody way
   on our altar at Mass.

Through the offering of Jesus
   we have hope of obtaining Your forgiveness
   and the graces we need to save our souls.

In the Consecration we give You
   the best Gift we could offer—your own Son:
   to adore and thank You,
   to ask Your pardon, and to beg for Your help.

And in Holy Communion You give us
   your best Gift—Your own Son as the Bread
      of Life.
   Before going to the Holy Table
   to receive this Food for our souls,
   we pray: "Father, give us this day our Daily
      Bread."

Jesus is our Daily Bread in Holy Communion.

THE
HAIL MARY

The words of the Angel Gabriel:

Hail Mary, full of grace!
The Lord is with thee.

The words of Saint Elizabeth:

Blessed art thou among women,
and blessed is the fruit
of thy womb, Jesus.

The words of the Church:

Holy Mary, Mother of God.
pray for us sinners,
now and at the hour of our death.
Amen.

The Blessed Virgin has a special love for children. 21

Hail Mary, Full of Grace!

MARY, my Mother,
the Angel Gabriel
said to you:

"Hail, full of grace!
The Lord is with you."

You are called "full of grace"
because God poured His
richest graces upon you.

**The Angel Gabriel says to Mary: "Hail, full of grace!
The Lord is with you."**

The Lord Is with Thee

MARY, my Mother, the Angel Gabriel also
said, "The Lord is with you."

The Lord was with you in a wonderful way,
not only by His grace and power,
but as your Son.

When you answered the angel with the words:
"I am the servant of the Lord.
Let it be done to me as you say,"
the Son of God became man in your womb.
The Lord was with you for nine months as
your Child.
resting under your heart.

Each time I say the Hail Mary,
I remind you of this most wonderful honor
of being the Mother of God,
and I thank God with you for all He has done
for you.

24   **Mary visits Elizabeth who greets her with joy.**

Blessed Art Thou
Among Women

MARY, my Mother, when the Angel had
gone away,
   you at once made a journey to visit your
   cousin Elizabeth.

When Elizabeth heard your greeting,
   she was filled with the Holy Spirit and cried
      out:
   "Blest are you among women
   and blest is the fruit of your womb.
   But who am I that the mother of my Lord
   should come to me?"

Mary, you knew that you were great and holy
   only because of God's love for you.
   You knew that you owed everything to His
      mercy.

And Blessed Is the Fruit of Thy Womb, Jesus

M ARY, my Mother, how wonderful
    was your visit to your cousin Elizabeth!

The Holy Spirit let Elizabeth know
  that the Son of God was already under your
    heart.
  The "Fruit" of your womb was Jesus, the Son
    of God,
  worthy of the praises of human beings
  and Angels for all eternity.

Mary, your Son is the Way, the Truth, and the
    Life—the Redeemer of the world.
  The name of Jesus means "Savior."

Your Son saved His people from their sins
  by shedding His Blood on the Cross.
  Through the name of Jesus we are saved,
  and we have hope of eternal life with God.

In saying the Hail Mary,
  I want to join you, Mary, in thanking God
  for all He has done for you,
  and through you, for all human beings.

Holy Mary, Mother of God

MARY, my Mother, I honor you as the Mother of God.
I believe that Jesus Christ is God.
Since you gave birth to Jesus,
you are truly the Mother of God.

With Joseph, Mary adores her new-born Son Jesus. 27

Pray for Us Sinners

MARY, my Mother,
from the Cross Jesus gave to your care
the souls He was redeeming.
He said to you, "Woman, there is your son."
Then He said to the disciple John,
who took our place beneath the Cross:
"There is your mother."

We have sinned against God,
and Jesus died to take away our sins
and to open heaven for all of us sinners.
You wanted to do His Last Will,
especially by being a Mother to all of us.
You are the Mother of us sinners.

Mary, you are called
"The Refuge of Sinners,"
because you are the Mother of the Good
Shepherd
who laid down His life for His sheep.
Pray for us sinners, your children.

From the Cross Jesus gives us His Mother.

Now and at the Hour of Our Death. Amen.

MARY, my Mother, we need your help
above all at the hour of our death,
the hour of our greatest need,
because on your help depends an eternity of
joy.

When God called Joseph to heaven,
Jesus and you were at his side.
He loved and served you so faithfully.
Now he died happily in your arms.

Mary, stand at my bedside when I am dying.
Help me in my last moments.
Protect me from the enemy,
and obtain for me a happy death,
and the glory of heaven.

You are my most powerful friend
before Jesus, the Just Judge,
to whom you can pray for me
with the unfailing prayers of a mother.

Pray that I may prepare for death
by living a holy life on earth with your help.

JESUS, Mary, Joseph,
  I give you my heart and my soul.

Jesus, Mary, Joseph,
help me in my last agony.

Jesus, Mary, Joseph,
may I die in peace with you.

Joseph dies in the care of Jesus and Mary.

The "GLORY BE TO THE FATHER"

The Holy Trinity

AFTER the *Our Father* and the *Hail Mary* there is perhaps no more important prayer for every Catholic to say than the prayer of praise to the Blessed Trinity, the *Glory be to the Father.* This prayer reminds us that there are three Persons in one God, that each Person has showed His love for us, and therefore deserves praise forever. Many times a day, say:

> Glory be to the Father,
> and to the Son
> and to the Holy Spirit.

> As it was in the beginning,
> is now, and ever shall be,
> world without end. Amen.